I'm Reading About

ALASKA

The Last Frontier!

GALLOPADE

by Carole Marsh

Printed and Manufactured in Peachtree City, GA., USA
www.gallopade.com

Book design: John Hanson

Editorial manager: Janice Baker

Alaska is a great state.
It is one of a kind.

What makes Alaska special?
Let's read about it
and see!

NATIVE AMERICANS

Who lived in Alaska first?

Native Americans did!

They moved around to find food.
They hunted in Alaska's woods.
They fished in Alaska's rivers.
They gathered fruits and seeds and nuts.

EXPLORERS

The first explorers came to Alaska in 1741.
They came from the country of Russia.

Vitus Jonassen Bering was their leader.
He and his men were looking for new land!

SETTLEMENT

A man named Grigory Shelikhov came
to Alaska from Russia.
He started the first settlement in Alaska.
He named it Three Saints Bay.

Three Saints Bay was on Kodiak Island.
It was a trading center for animal furs.

Three Saints Bay

STATEHOOD

Alaska was the 49th state
to join the United States of America!

Isn't it great,
to be a state!
I bet Alaska
could hardly wait!

Alaska became a state in 1959.

Alaska The 49th State

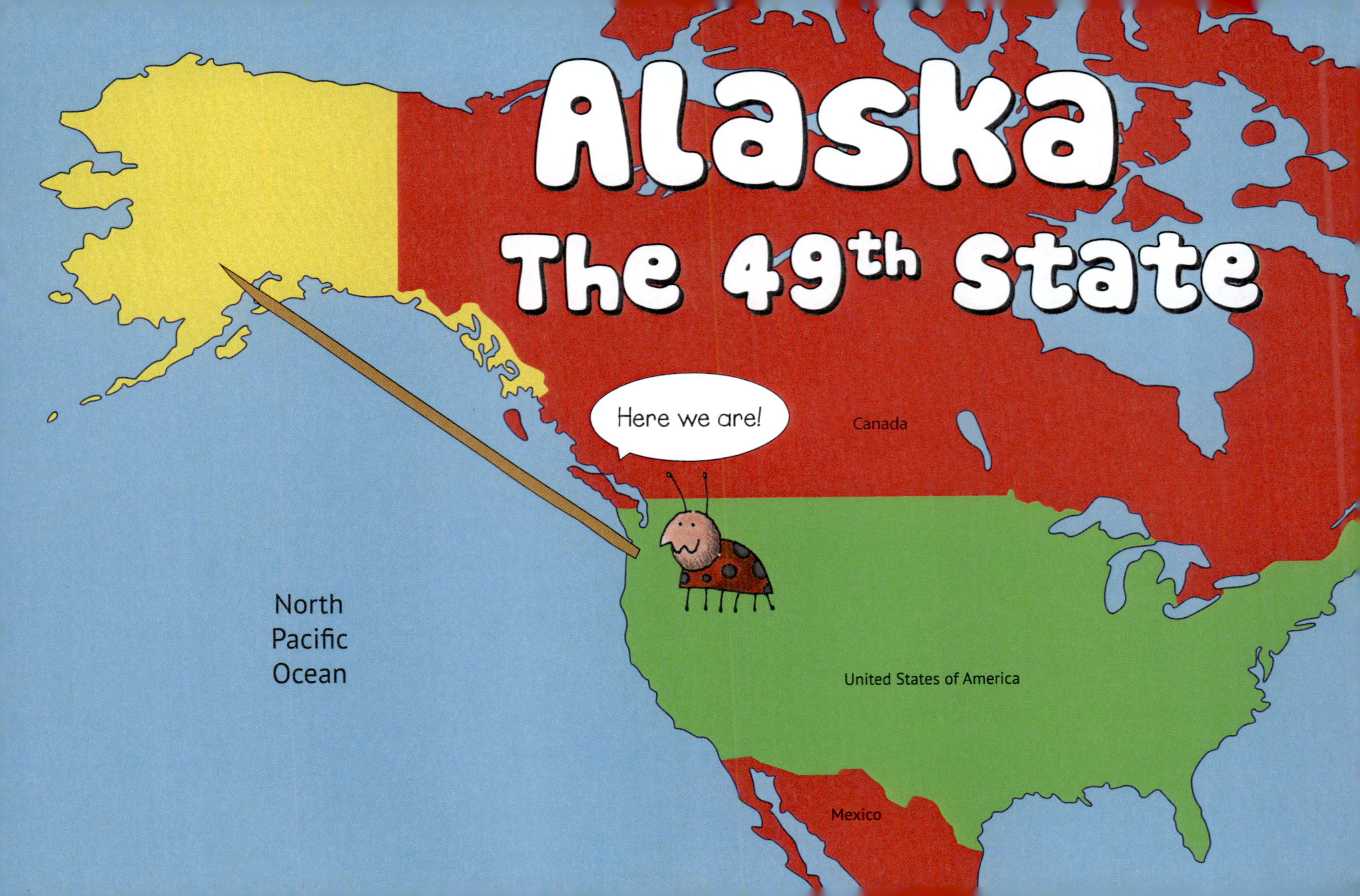

FLAG

I am the state flag.
I was adopted in 1927.

What color am I?
I am blue.

Look at me.
What else do you see?

I fly high over the state of Alaska!

CAPITAL

Say hello to Juneau,
the capital city of Alaska!

There is an important building in Juneau.
It is the State Capitol.
Alaska's laws are made there!

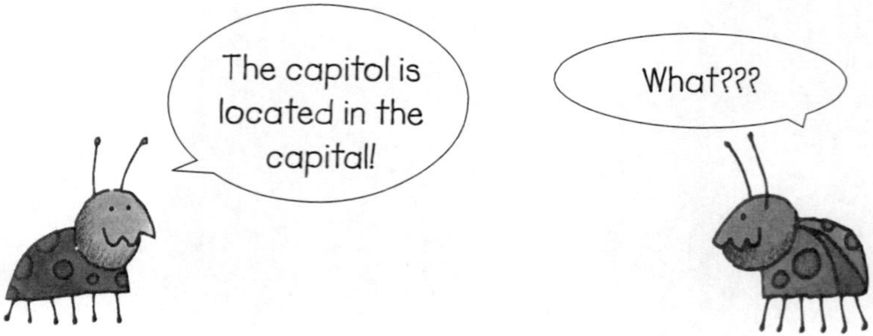

Capitol

SEAL

I am a seal,
but I am not the State Seal.
If I were, I would be very important.
I would be stamped on many official papers.
(Ouch, that might hurt!)

THE SEAL OF THE STATE
OF ALASKA

Now, that's official!

NICKNAME

State nicknames are fun!
State nicknames are great!
They share fun facts
about each state!

Alaska's nickname is "The Last Frontier."

Why is Alaska called "The Last Frontier"?
Alaska is a huge state with many places still to explore!

The Last Frontier

BORDERS

Look at Alaska.
Alaska is north of the continental United States.

Alaska borders the country of Canada.
Find Alaska and its neighbor on the map!

Borders

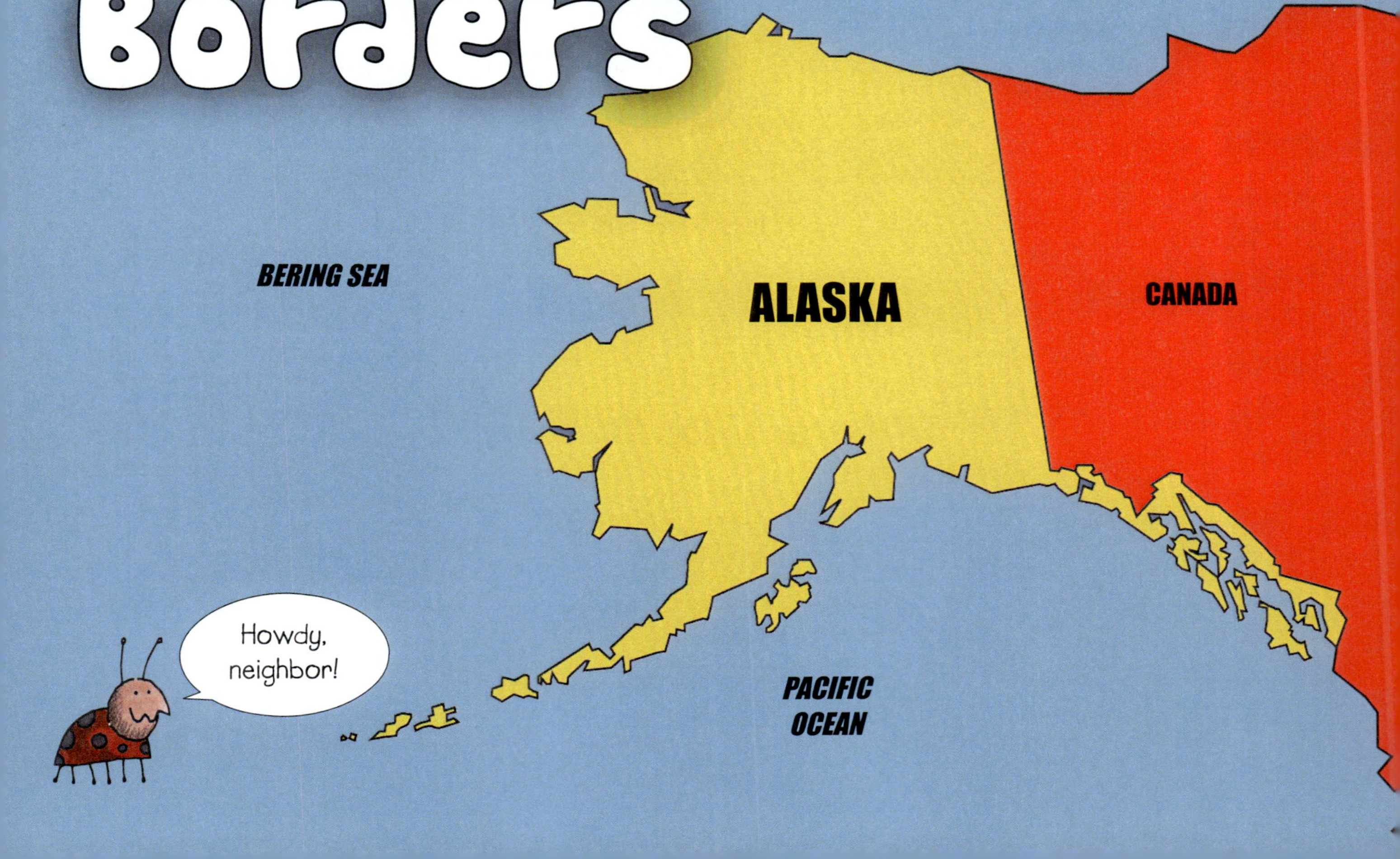

BOROUGHS

Alaska is divided into boroughs.
Boroughs are a form of local government.
Boroughs provide services that people need!
Those services include:

Schools **Libraries** **Police**

Firefighters **Road Repair** **and More!**

Boroughs

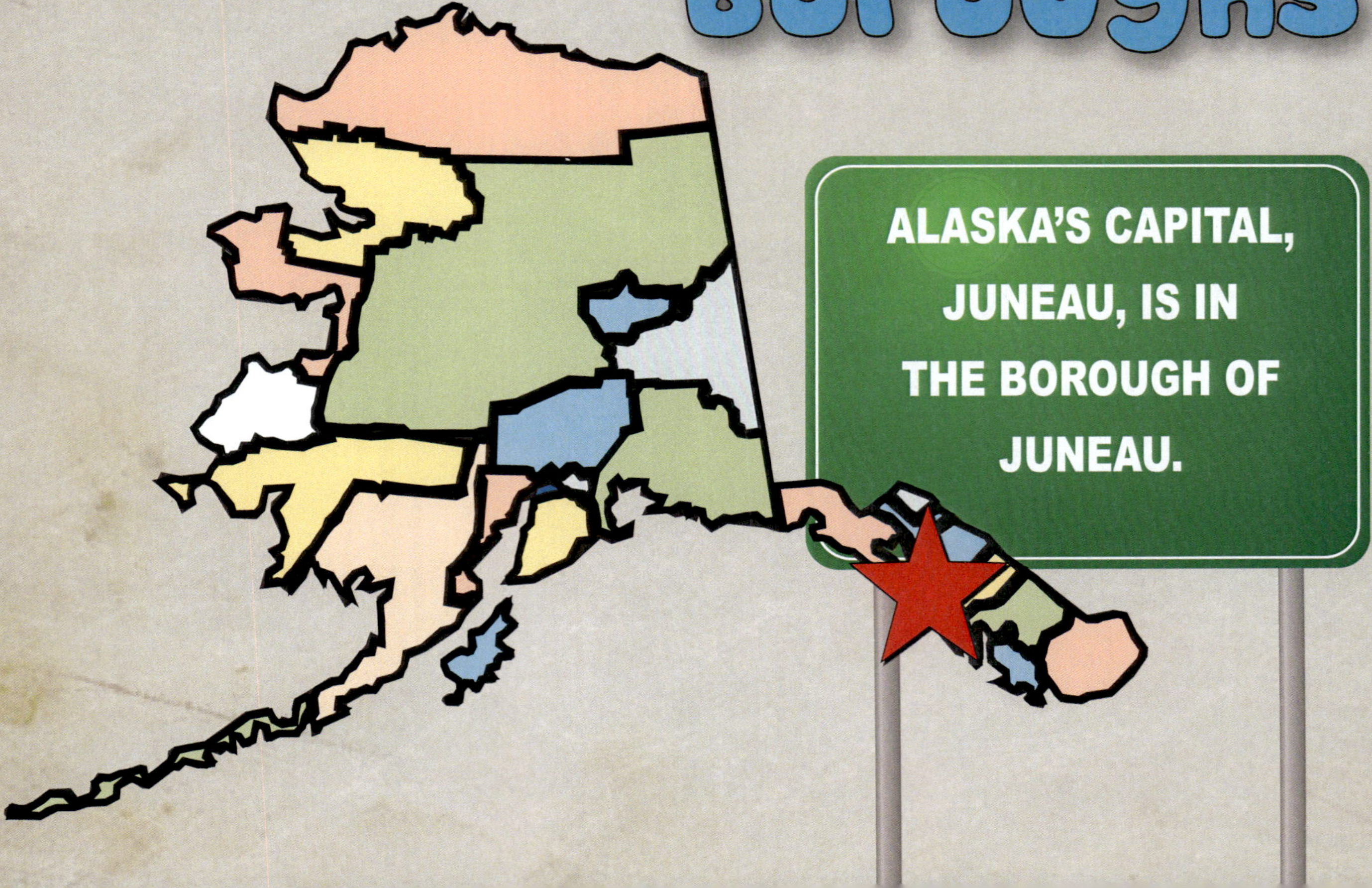

Many famous people

Benny Benson

Young boy who designed the Alaska flag

Elizabeth Peratrovich

Worked for equal rights for Alaska's native peoples

Libby Riddles

First woman to win the Iditarod Trail Sled Dog Race

call our state home!

Sarah Palin
First female governor of Alaska

Chad Carpenter
Cartoonist known for his comic strip *Tundra*

Tommy Moe
Olympic gold medal winner in downhill skiing

PEOPLE

Willow Ptarmigan

BIRD

I am the state bird, and I fly
over Alaska, proud and high.

As I fly, up in the sky,
I flap my wings to tell you "Hi!"

The Alaska state bird is the Willow Ptarmigan.

Forget-me-not

FLOWER

I am the Forget-me-not.
I am the state flower.

I grow where it's warm and sunny.
I bloom in spring and summer.
I help make Alaska beautiful!

Look at me! Smell me!
My blooms are a beautiful
blue color!

Sitka Spruce

TREE

I am a Sitka Spruce—I'm the state tree.
Southeastern and central Alaska is where to find me.

My roots run deep, they keep me strong.
My leaves stay green, all year long.

I stand up straight, big and tall.
Don't climb too high—it would hurt to fall!

Four-Spot Skimmer Dragonfly

INSECT

I am the Four-Spot Skimmer Dragonfly.
I am the state insect.

I flit and I fly over rivers and lakes.
I like living near water.

Look at my body and wings.
What colors do you see?

Islands

ISLANDS

Let's go to an island!

Alaska has over 2,000 islands.
Some are big. Some are small.

Some islands have trees that
cover them in green.
Some islands have no trees at all.

Alaska's islands are home to many animals:

Sea Otters **Sea Lions** **Walrus** **Whales** **Birds** **and More!**

Mountains

MOUNTAINS

Alaska's magnificent mountains are the place to be.
Hiking and camping—
fun for you and me.

Winter weather brings lots of snow.
Temperatures drop to freezing and below!

Rivers

RIVERS

Alaska has many rivers.
People like to use rivers for boating and fishing!

This habitat is home to many animals:

Bear Birds Moose Fish Caribou and More!

Alaskan rivers are known for great salmon fishing!

Chilkoot Trail

The Chilkoot Trail is a hiking trail in Alaska!
It was once used by gold miners.
They hiked the long trail to get to the Yukon goldfields.
The hike was very difficult!

People still hike the Chilkoot Trail today.
They have to watch out for bad weather and bears!

LANDMARK

Alaska Crops

Alaska has many farms.
Why?
Because Alaska has good soil and lots of sunlight in the summer!

Some of the top crops grown in Alaska are:

Nursery Plants **Hay** **Oats** **Potatoes**

Sports in Alaska

SPORTS

Basketball! Hockey! Skiing!
Alaska has it all.

Whether you like to watch or play,
You are sure to have a ball!

Seawolves **Nanooks**

Aces

& More!

Alaska: Home of the Aurora Borealis

CLAIM TO FAME

You can see the Aurora Borealis in Fairbanks!

The Aurora Borealis is also called the Northern Lights.
It is a wave of blue, green, and purple lights
in the night sky.
Auroras are only visible near
the North and South Poles.

The best time to see the Aurora Borealis is during the dark winter.

GLOSSARY

caribou: a large North American reindeer

frontier: unsettled land

habitat: a place where plants or animals naturally live

island: a piece of land surrounded by water

laws: rules made by the government

magnificent: impressively beautiful; superb

settlement: the first community in an area

visible: to be able to be seen